FROM COURAGE TO COURTESY

TO COURTESY

Soft Skills and Etiquette
Tips for the Fire Service

MARLA HARR

ISBN: 978-0-9968674-0-5

First Printing: March, 2018

Published by 102nd Place LLC
Scottsdale, AZ 85266

Illustrations by: Azalea Patricia Rodriguez
www.AzaleaPatricia.weebly.com

Dedication

This book is dedicated to all the fire fighters and EMTs who work tirelessly to serve their communities.

June 10, 2005 my sister's house caught fire and was a total loss. The good news – it happened during the day so the family was safe. The fire fighters were so kind and tried so hard to save items. It was their sincere concern and professionalism that helped my family through that devastating day.

To the EMTs who responded twice to our 911 calls when mom was having minor strokes. They quickly got her to the hospital for a full recovery.

Our family will always be grateful to the Fire Service. Thank you.

The Guerra Family

MaryAnn, Marla, Michael, Diana, Joe, and Anne

Table of Contents

INTRODUCTION

"Culture shock – the feeling of shock or of being disoriented which someone has when they experience a different and unfamiliar culture."
~ Richard D. Lewis, from his book:
When Cultures Collide

Culture shock is what I experienced each time my career advanced. It is also what I've found through my training and coaching that everyone experiences when they take on a new role. It is what you should expect too as you move through the ranks in fire service.

Let me give you a few examples of what it means to experience culture shock in your professional life. At one point in my career I was working in the training and development department of human resources for a major retail company. I had just been promoted to lead the testing, training, and installation of a new point-of-sale system. It was exciting to get a chance to work with the Data Processing team on this major project. My first meeting with my new teammates was culture shock.

Although we were in the same building and with the same company, the data center felt like a totally different world. They spoke a language I didn't understand, even though the words were in English. They had a different dress code, different work hours, and a different office protocol. What I knew and was familiar with from Human Resources wouldn't work here. Fortunately, a software engineer named Michael saw that I was floundering and took me under his wing. He became my mentor for learning this new language and culture.

When I left retail and went into the event management industry I got another dose of culture shock. Once again the language was different – event management had its own set of jargon and buzz words. But even more pronounced were the differences I found when putting on events across the United States. I had no idea we as a nation have so many distinct ways of speaking English i.e. soda in the East is pop in the Midwest is Coke in the South regardless of the type of soft drink. What is acceptable behavior in one region of the country is totally unacceptable in another. Working with companies in New York City was very different than working with companies in New Orleans.

In both of these situations I had to make changes to my approach, be open to learning new languages, and embracing the differences in others and the way they do business in order to build relationships. To be successful in my career I knew I had to adapt to new ways of doing business. They were not going to adapt to me.

For the past fifteen years I've been training professionals, mainly from corporations, on the etiquette skills they need to continue to be successful. A Fire Chief happened to attend one of my talks. Afterwards he approached me and commented that he would love to see a book like this specifically for those in the fire service. He let me know how unique the needs were because as one moves up the ranks they are no longer expected to deal with only those within the fire service. There are unions, governments, business people, and average citizens with whom they need to interact and communicate effectively. All of them have their own unique languages, customs, environments, and culture.

Being in the fire service is often a legacy. Many of you have grown up in a home and extended family where dad, brothers, uncles, and grandfathers were all fire fighters. Now we can add moms, sisters, aunts, and grandmothers to this legacy. The fire service culture becomes your world; the people around you speak the same language, same ethics, morals and code of conduct. The fire house has its own set of rules, acceptable behaviors, protocols and etiquette. Even the fire truck has a set of rules and language. Each person has specific duties that have to be performed to the protocols of their position because in many cases we're talking about life and death situations.

But let's face it, most union, government, or business jobs do not entail life and death situations, hence the reason for this book. The training and mind-set of someone in the fire service is different from those in business organizations. The transition from the fire house to conducting business with outside industries can be overwhelming and frustrating. It's "culture shock" and you need to know how to understand others and develop a new set of behaviors and skills that will give you the confidence and professional savvy to be successful in the world outside the fire service.

From Courage to Courtesy is based on five easy to understand and execute principles to aid you in adapting to the inevitable culture shock.

- Cultural differences of language, environment, view of time/work hours
- Chain of command for each organization. Who will you contact? Who makes the decisions?
- Cultivating the relationship
- Communication types and styles
- Public speaking
- Code of behaviors and soft skills needed for transition

If you're reading this book I know that you are motivated to learn, have a willingness to adapt to changing environments, and are open to other business cultures. Bravo! Take it step-by-step and these new ways of thinking and behaving will soon become as natural as responding to an alarm.

To your success!

Marla Harr

PHYSICAL POWER POINTS

We are constantly communicating from the moment we wake up to the moment we lay our heads on our pillow at the end of the day. We speak through our writing, text or a formal letter. We speak through our voices in face-to-face conversations, voice messages, or on the phone. We speak through our physical body, i.e. our eyes, forehead, and facial expression, our handshake, posture and our dress. It's important to realize that when we are awake we are always communicating and sending out messages.

Stepping out of the fire house culture into other types of organizations does require a more formal approach than you may have in the fire service. This is especially true if you are meeting someone for the first time. Remember you have about five seconds to make your first impression. In this chapter we are going to look at six power points that send out both physical as well as non-physical messages.

"The face is a picture of the mind as the eyes are its interpreter."   Cicero (106-43 B.C.)

Number 1 – The Eyes Have It

Our eyes convey important unspoken messages. They show if you are listening to the person with whom you are in a conversation. They:

- Show how interested you are in the conversation.
- Tell the other person a bit about your personality.

Eye contact is important in business and vital if you are to present yourself with confidence and poise. You need to know and understand the signals you are sending with your eyes, and equally important, you need to be aware of the eye signals of others.

Our true feelings are expressed primarily in the upper face, through the eyes, brows and forehead. This is the "business" eye contact zone.

Eye Signals – Business

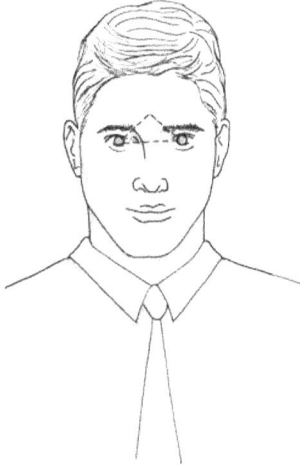

Notice the triangle is centered on the eyes, eyebrows and forehead. Studies have shown that true feelings and emotions are expressed mainly in the upper part of your face. By keeping your gaze most of the time in this triangle it does several things:

A. Tells the other person that you are listening and actually makes you a better listener.

B. Helps you to be aware of the signals the other person is sending as well as your own.

C. Helps you to focus attention on the person you're talking to and makes them feel important while you look self-confident.

D. Creates a more business like impression.

What do your eyes reveal?

Eye Signals - Social

A gaze below the eye level suggests a social atmosphere is developing. Become aware of the location of your own gaze as this is not professional. Some people may be uncomfortable if they think you are staring at their nose, mouth or chin, particularly if they are not happy with these parts of their face.

In business a good rule to follow is to keep direct eye contact at 40 to 60 percent while engaged in conversation. Two important points about direct eye contact:

First – When used less than 40-60 percent, you may appear to be shy, shifty, hiding something, or lacking in self-confidence.

Think about a time when you were in a conversation and the person constantly kept looking around – at the door, at other people, out the window, etc. How did that make you feel? I'm betting a bit uncomfortable and that you and the conversation were not important.

Second - If you hold your gaze too long (more than 60%) you may make the person feel that they are on the spot, that you're being condescending or even intimidating.

Again, how do you feel when someone is keeping their focus on you and not adjusting their direct eye contact? It can be an unnerving and uncomfortable feeling.

When you are talking, watch your listener's eyes to see if you are holding their attention. If the person you're talking to isn't listening it doesn't matter what you are saying!

Hot Tip: Keep your eyes in the business area [eyes, brows, forehead] 40-60 percent of the conversation time.

Remember, when your job responsibilities begin to move you outside the fire service to interact with other organizations, the building of relationships will be different than you may be used to. Understanding the power of your eye contact can boost your self-confidence, professional image, and career success.

Number 2 – Step into the Spotlight

The type of entrance you make in attending any business function is so important. In fact, it's vital if you are to present yourself with confidence and poise.

You might be asking yourself, "Why?" That's a great question with a very simple answer. Most people watch the entrance to a room – any room – a conference room, a networking event in a hotel meeting room, or a restaurant. I think you get the picture.

Good news – this is a wonderful window of opportunity for you to make a positive impression. You may have heard it only takes five seconds to make an impression! That's an intimidating statistic but well researched and documented. Keep in mind we all do this; it's part of being human. What makes a great business entrance? Posture! It instantly creates the impression of a confident, capable person.

A. If you walk in with your head up, spine straight, and shoulders down and relaxed, you will look confident, self-assured and in control.

B. If you walk in all stooped shoulders and looking down you'll come across as shy, lacking self-confidence, having low self-esteem, or being uncomfortable.

C. If you walk in with quite the strut you can come across as arrogant, overly confident and maybe someone others don't want to meet.

Good Posture   Poor Posture

Hot Tip: Five second rule – you have five seconds to make a first impression – make it a good one.

Now that you have the posture down what's next? A few more tips to aid you in looking confident:

1. Walk through the doorway and move to the right if right-handed or left if you are left-handed.

Never stop in the door where you are blocking the entrance – someone may be behind you.

You don't want anyone to run into you! That would not be the most graceful entrance.

2. Pause. It gives you the chance to spot key people, find a chair, or someone you know. You can head to a seat or a conversation with confidence. It allows people to see you before you mingle with others.

3. Always dress appropriately for the function you are attending. Dress is as important as posture in the five second impression you are creating for yourself. If you are not sure what is appropriate, ask the person who is putting on the meeting or event.

Hot Tip: Proper posture is the key. It instantly creates the sense of a confident person.

Number 3 – Handling the Handshake

Ever wonder where the ritual of handshaking began? In the book, *The Power of Handshaking*, authors Robert E. Brown and Dorothea Johnson had this to say:

> "*The ritual of shaking hands arose sometime during the Roman Empire, not out of courtesy and good will, but out of fear. The human past was one of danger, where wild*

beasts and bandits roamed and men walked around well-armed. All strangers immediately aroused suspicion . . .

In order to become friends, you first had to make sure the other man would not attack. You either laid down your weapons or kept your right (dominant) hands away from them, displaying empty palms. (Because left-handedness was considered evil in those days, you exposed right hands.) To be certain, neither of you would grab his sword and lunge, you grasped right hands. Thus the handshake was born – not of friendship but of mistrust."

Today the western handshake has become a universal, non-verbal form of greeting and communication. A handshake reveals many things about you or the person with whom you are shaking hands. It can show personality, feelings, motivation, and attitude toward others. In essence a handshake is communication that doesn't require an explanation and is not often misunderstood.

You are judged by your handshake and you make judgments about others when you shake their hand.

> **Hot Tip:** When conducting international business learn the proper handshake or greeting for that country. This is a positive and appropriate gesture in building relationships.

Here are the steps that ensure a commanding handshake:

1. Right hand – should always be free, ready to shake hands.
2. Left hand – hold only one item, you don't want to be fumbling with items if you need your right hand free to shake hands.
3. Extend hand thumb up and fingers out, this allows the other person's hand to connect with yours for a genuine handshake.

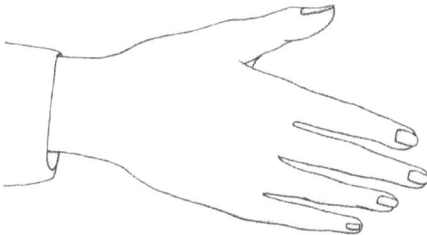

4. Connect hands – web-to-web – this is the area between your thumb and index finger.
5. Shake from the elbow – not the wrist or shoulder.
6. Two smooth pumps – then release hands.

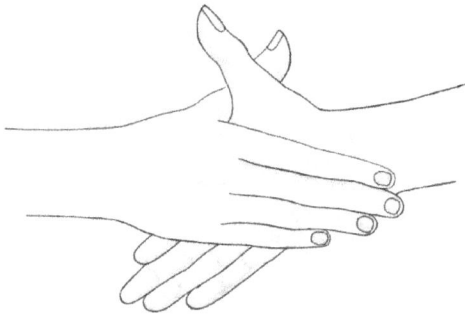

A few extra tips:

- Stand facing the individual with your shoulders squared to theirs. This allows you to see the person's face and name badge. Be sure to look them in the eye, smile and call them by name. Use titles if appropriate.
- Name badge – goes on your right shoulder so people can easily see your name as they're shaking your hand.

Most people tend to place the badge on the left shoulder, or with men, on the breast pocket of their suit. This is incorrect.

- Avoid thumb down, fingers curled – this does not allow for a solid grasp.
- Clammy hands control – spray/rub clear antiperspirant on your palms.
- Avoid fragrance – use it sparingly, many people are allergic to fragrance.
- Avoid large rings – they can interfere with the proper grip and can be painful if your hand is squeezed too hard.
- Awareness alert – be attentive to others with a disability.

- In the United States there is no set rule for who offers a hand first. The person who does extend their hand first benefits as this establishes that they are comfortable taking the initiative, are not timid, and have self-confidence – all pluses in making a good impression.
- A woman who extends her hand first removes any hesitation a man might have in offering his hand.

Hot Tip: Handshaking rule – gender doesn't matter in western business; both men and women use the same handshake.

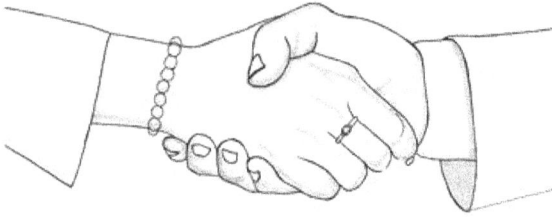

You shake hands when:

- Someone enters your office or home.
- You meet someone outside your office or home.
- You enter a room and are greeted by those you know, or are introduced to someone you don't know.
- Leave a gathering or say good-bye to an individual.
- Congratulating someone who won an award or gave a speech.
- Consoling someone.
- Concluding a business transaction or contract.

Handshaking Internationally
- Know the correct greeting for that nation before you go.
- The Western handshake is accepted

throughout the world in business today. As relationships are built, be aware that the formal western handshake may be replaced with a culture's accepted greeting. For example, in the Middle East (Arab) when men are conducting business the custom is for them to embrace and kiss on both cheeks. Men do not shake hands with women in the Middle East.

- Outside the United States, inter-national protocol is that you shake hands with everyone in a group. Don't stop halfway with a "hello everyone" wave to the rest of the people. This is deemed a rejection by those you omitted and everyone notices.

- Shake hands when you arrive and depart. Your grip should be firm, never hard; it may be lighter in some cultures.

- Stay away from the fingertip hand-shake; it's unpopular around the world.

- Women in some cultures do not touch a man in business so a handshake is unacceptable. Know this before you go and instead give a simple smile and verbal greeting.

Number 4 – First Class Introductions

We make ourselves known by how we introduce ourselves and others. Often times it's difficult to go up and meet new people or a company executive. The thing to remember is you are not alone! Many new and recently promoted employees are unsure of the correct etiquette and protocol so the natural instinct is to delay or wait for someone else to step in and make the introductions. Good news – learning how to do a "first class" introduction is an easy behavior skill to master and incorporate into your everyday actions.

What to say when introducing yourself to generate a first class image:

"Hi," is defiantly not enough.

"Hello," is a better word but again not enough in business.

"Hello, I'm Deacon Richards." Better but not quite there yet.

"Hello, I'm Deacon Richards, with the Phoenix Fire Service." Almost there.

"Hello, I'm Deacon Richards, Fire Chief, city of Phoenix." This is a great self-introduction!

Why? Because Deacon has given his full name, his position (helps others to understand role and responsibilities), and the fire service he represents. In business this is the type of information you need to start a conversation and establish connections.

Take accountability and introduce yourself when:

- You recognize someone and they don't recognize you – always put the other person at ease and mention where you previously met.
- Attend any meeting, networking, or business function.
- You are seated next to a stranger – don't wait for them, be polite and introduce yourself. This will break the ice and help start the conversation.
- The person introducing you forgets your name – help them out and say your name. We have all, at one time or another, forgotten a person's name. We know how uncomfortable that can be.

Hot Tip: Introduce yourself – it's your responsibility and the professional thing to do.

When another has introduced you to someone new, your response can say a lot about you. Responding to introductions:

- "Hello." Sounds too immature for business.
- "Hello, it's a pleasure to meet you Mr. Jones." Excellent! Using the person's name helps you to remember their name.

When the person who introduced you did not use your title or company name, be sure to include it in your response. By repeating your name, title, and company it helps to reinforce it for Mr. Jones.

Protocol for Business Introductions:

The titles that follow are used in the private sector to help you understand the chain of command in most of these organizations. The same formula is used in government, military, fire, and police services. You need to use the correct title for the established hierarchy in each sector.

When you are not sure of a person's title or the hierarchy do your due diligence and look it up using Google to search for the person's name or search for the organization chart for that company, city, state, department, etc. Organization charts will not have a person's name however it will show positions and ranking within the organization. Gotta love Google!!

- Who will be introduced to whom is determined by their rank or position within the organization. The person who holds the highest position takes priority over others who work there.
- Elected officials and the military also have rank and position status.

Formula for Introductions
- Higher Position *(President, Vice President, Director, etc.)* RECEIVES Lower Position *(Manger, Sales Person, new associate)*. By RECEIVE I mean the lower level position person is introduced "to" the higher level person.

Order of Introductions:
1. Junior executive or associate is introduced to the Senior executive. Non-official person is introduced to the elected Official person.

2. Company executive or associate is introduced to the Client. Note: Company executives being introduced to the client seems strange to some people. The rule is simple – without clients you would not have a business. Clients take precedence!

For an easy way to remember how to introduce someone it's useful to think of two music images. One is the "Happy Birthday" song and the other is the rock group "U2."

Correct is The Happy Birthday Song – think happy birthday **"to you."** Incorrect is the Rock group U2 – think **"you to."**

For example, Mary is going to introduce her new employee John Smith to the president of the company Mr. Anderson.

Incorrect: "Mr. Anderson, I would like <u>you to</u> meet John Smith, our new manager in accounting."

Correct: "Mr. Anderson, I would like to introduce <u>to you</u> John Smith, our new manager in accounting."

Elected officials have titles. Be sure to use them correctly.

The President of the United States
Conversation: Mr. President or Sir
"How do you do Mr. President?"
"Good morning/afternoon/evening, Sir."

The Wife of the President of the United States
Conversation: Mrs. Doe
"How do you do Mrs. Doe?"

The Vice President of the United States

Conversation: Mr. Vice President or Sir
"How do you do Mr. Vice President?"
"Good morning/afternoon/evening, Sir."

The Wife of the Vice President of the United States

Conversation: Mrs. Smith
"How do you do Mrs. Smith?"

United States Senator

Conversation: Senator or Senator Brown
"How do you do Senator Brown?"
"Good morning/afternoon/evening, Senator."

United States Representative

Conversation: Mr. Giles or Ms. Giles
"How do you do Mr. Giles?"
"Good morning/afternoon/evening, Ms. Giles."

Note: A member of the United States House of Representatives should *never* be addressed as Representative Doe, *except when introducing*.

For example: When introducing a U.S. House Representative you may say, "The Honorable Mary Doe, Representative from Ohio."

Never use the term Congressman or Congresswoman in your introduction as this term can indicate either a Senator or a Representative of the House and can be confusing.

Governor
Conversation: Governor Jones or Governor
"How do you do Governor Jones?" "Good morning/afternoon/evening, Governor."

State Senator/State Representative
Refer to the above - same as United States Senator or United States House Representative.

Mayor
Conversation: Mayor Rush or Mayor
"How do you do Mayor Rush?"
"Good morning/afternoon/evening, Mayor."

Judge (not in the Supreme Court)
Conversation: Judge Quinn or Judge
"How do you do Judge Quinn?"
"Good morning/afternoon/evening, Judge."

Protestant Minister (with a Doctor's degree)
Conversation: Dr. Morales, Sir, or Madam
"How do you do Sir/Madam/Dr. Morales?"
"Good morning/afternoon/evening, Sir, Madam, Dr. Morales."

Catholic Priest or Nun
Conversation: Father or Father Lee
"How do you do Father?"
"Good morning/afternoon/ evening

Father Lee."

Conversation: Sister or Sister Mary
"How do you do Sister?"
"Good morning/afternoon/ evening,
Sister Mary."

Rabbi
Conversation: Rabbi or Rabbi Cohen
"How do you do Rabbi Cohen?"
"Good morning/afternoon/ evening,
Rabbi."

Note: The above introduction material is taken from
Outclass The Competition - Business Etiquette by The
Protocol School of Washington® Copyright© 1995-
2006.

Hot Tip: A higher level executive receives a
lower level employee.

Hints and Tips:
- Unnecessary gestures – keep hands
  low, don't pull people together.
- Look at each person.
- You are introduced in error – correct
  immediately in a positive tone of voice.
- Your firm is misidentified – correct
  immediately in a positive tone of voice.

- Always stand – the only two exceptions are a disability or the position of your seat makes it difficult to stand.

Social Events A Few More Tips:
- Eat a small amount of food before you go.
- Key persons – know who you should meet and who can introduce you.
- Peers – make yourself known to those you do know.
- Join a conversation – skillfully join into a conversation. A networking event is designed for people to meet new people so don't be shy about entering into a group of attendees. Catch the eye of one of the group members and simply ask if you can join. "Do you mind if I join your group?" Chances are they are going to say something like "please do." Be sure to introduce yourself properly with your name, position and company.
- Shake hands and do it with everyone in a group.

Number 5 – Do Sweat the Small Talk

There is an interesting study from Harvard University, The Carnegie Foundation and Stanford Research Institute. They found that

85% of your job success is based on your people or "soft" skills and not your technical knowledge of your job responsibilities. Soft skills are your ability to get along and work well with others.

Your people skills determine if you:

- Will, or will not get a job.
- Be retained or let go from a job.
- Passed over or given the promotion.

Hot Tip: Our people skills are the prime qualities that make and keep us employed.

Let's talk small talk – it's an important people skill because it:
- Breaks the ice – helps to make others more comfortable.
- Establishes a connection – helps to build relationships.
- Doesn't require original or profound conversation – it's "chit-chat."
- Is the polite thing to do – it's part of showing good manners.

In order to excel at small talk you need to:
- Be well-informed – keep up with what is going on locally, nationally, and internationally.

- Focus on the other person – ask open-ended questions, learn about them.
- Don't interrupt – sometimes this is hard to do but always allow a person to complete their thought.
- Do listen – keep your focus on the other person and what they are saying.
- Think before you speak – once you say something you can't take it back.
- Close a conversation – always end the conversation. Example: "It's been a pleasure talking with you Mary," or "Mary, I look forward to talking with you next week."

There are certain subjects that are best to stay clear of:
- Political issues
- Religion
- Your health or diet habits
- Cost of things
- Personal questions – For example: asking if someone is still married or is the divorce final, asking how much they paid for their house or car, etc.
- Mean gossip
- Off-color jokes
- Any issue that could be considered controversial

Number 6 – How to Use Your Business Card

How you present and use your business card is an important part in building professional relationships. Your card represents you and the organization you represent. It should be given to someone in a way that it is remembered and kept instead of tossed as soon as you turn your back.

Follow these first class business card etiquette Dos and Don'ts.

Dos for Business Card Etiquette

1. Present the card with the print facing the recipient so they will not have to turn it around to read it.
2. When receiving a card, take the time to look at it. A card is representative of the person and doing so shows respect.
3. Pay attention to the conversation and write pertinent notes on the card later.
4. Carry cards in a card case to keep them fresh and protected.
5. Before attending an event, always put a supply of cards in your suit pocket for easy access. Keep them in the right pocket and place cards you receive in the left pocket. You don't want to get your card mixed up with those you have accepted.

6. Present your business card to the receptionist each time you visit a company. It helps the receptionist announce you.

7. Carry business cards at social events in case a good business contact presents itself. However be discreet if cards are exchanged, especially in a private home.

Don'ts for Business Card Etiquette

1. Don't give out a business card that is defective, out of date, or soiled.

2. Don't pass out your cards like flyers. You will appear pushy and unprofessional if you are handing your card out indiscriminately.

3. Don't force your card on anyone.

4. Don't offer your card early in a conversation. Wait to see if there is a good business connection first.

5. Junior executives in the same firm don't give cards to, or request cards from, senior executives. Allow the senior executive to request your card or offer theirs.

6. Don't leave a person's card on the table. Take the card with you and dispose of it at your home or office if you're not interested.

> **Hot Tip:** Your business card is an important part of your marketing materials; keep them pristine.

Chapter in Review

Six important areas were covered: eye contact, the entrance, the handshake, proper introductions, small talk, and the business card. All of these will help you create a professional image of confidence and control. You can master these with practice and a commitment to becoming a truly polished professional.

BEYOND THE UNIFORM

"You never have a second chance to make a good first impression."
John T Molloy, Author of *Dress for Success*

This chapter is not to provide uniform guidelines for the fire service. Each state's fire service has its own protocols that determine the policies for each of the two types of dress uniform styles Class A and Class B. It would be too difficult to disclose them all here so I'll be giving an overview and what is required when you are appearing outside the fire service.

The dress uniform is a symbol of professionalism and honor. It is to be worn with dignity as it represents the fire service and the men and women who serve. The most common occasions where a dress uniform would be required are community events such as public or school speeches, parades, award ceremonies, , news media session, or a station grand opening. In addition, a dress uniform is often worn at funerals of community leaders, family, or friends.

Always consult with your superior if you are unsure of the proper dress when you are representing the department. Many have strict guidelines regarding specific functions or locations where a dress uniform can be worn. For example, you may not be allowed to wear it in a bar. Know your department's dress code policies.

So let's talk about what is acceptable dress in the business sector when you're not required to wear your dress uniform. This will ensure you dress appropriately for any business or social setting you may find yourself in. Unlike most other professions, as a fire fighter you are always representing the fire service.

In 1961, John Molloy became the first person to actively promote how you dress with how successful you become. His advice of suits and ties for men and skirted suits for women became the dressing "bible" for corporate America for almost 30 years.

Then the dot.com boom hit and suddenly wearing khakis was a career move. As the tech industry took off, white shirts and ties were replaced by polos and tees. Trousers became jeans or in some cases shorts. Everyone was trying to entice the Gen Y workforce.

The bubble burst in 2001 and since that time corporations have been moving steadily back toward a more traditional look. Even with "Casual Friday" or a "business casual" workplace, you are still judged by how you look. No matter how good you are at your job, how you dress can affect career advancement.

Taking it to the Street

Stepping out from your culture of a required dress code can be daunting. Showing up to a meeting or social event wearing something inappropriate can make you feel uncomfortable and uneasy. Let's face it, when we don't feel good about our appearance we don't perform as well.

If you are unsure of the dress then ask the person who invited you. It's always a safe bet to go conservative, better to be over-dressed than underdressed. Here are some guidelines you can follow.

Dressing for Men
- Short-sleeved shirts with ties are never appropriate unless you are an airline pilot – you'll look school-boyish. Even without ties they never look as professional as long-sleeved shirts.
- Ties should reach the top of your belt.

- Your belt should match the color of your shoes and so should your socks.
- In terms of suits, navy promotes authority and grey is more approachable. But not light grey – it will never look expensive.
- If your trousers have belt loops then wear a belt, not suspenders.
- Shoes should be thin-soled, lace-ups with a suit.

Dressing for Women
- Matching suits are no longer necessary to project a professional appearance but they are still required under some circumstances. Know your environment.
- Women's styles change frequently so your shoes should be updated every six months. Heels no higher than 2 to 2 ½ inches and color should be no lighter than your hemline.
- Skirts should be knee-length.
- Express your personality through the blouses you match with your suits – but always avoid loud prints.
- If nylons are required, make sure they are free of snags and runs.
- Navy, black, and grey can be worn year-round.

> **Hot Tip:** Buy the most expensive clothes and accessories you can afford. Do not overlook your shoes – they are one of the first items to be judged.

Casual Attire and Corporate Events

There is a lot of confusion over "casual" attire in the workplace so you aren't alone if you often wonder what this means when you get an invitation with casual as the dress code. Casual does not mean you get to wear what you might wear on the weekend. It is never, ever your favorite pair of jeans with the knees ripped out or sweatpants of any kind.

Casual is putting together a wardrobe that maintains the respect and credibility you deserve.

- Don't mix your looks i.e. wearing a quality belt with casual shoes.
- A jacket always empowers a look but don't wear your suit jacket. Get a quality sports jacket that is single-breasted.
- Never leave your shirt untucked and make sure it is pressed.
- Avoid t-shirts, particularly those with logos.

- No sneakers.
- No strappy tops/dresses for women – minimize the amount of skin.

> **Hot Tip:** Always have a set of your Class A and B clothes laundered and ready for last minute or emergency meetings where a change into dress uniform would be required.

Clean and Crisp

Now that you understand how to dress, let's talk about how to groom. Whether or not you appear clean and fresh says a lot about the respect you have for others. Things like bad breath, smoking odors, and un-fresh clothes (body odor) will turn people off and keep you from putting your best foot forward. The impression you'll leave is "if he/she doesn't care about personal hygiene how much do they care about their work?"

So here are some things to think about before you leave the house:

- Hair should be clean and styled. If your hair is long (men and women) it should be tied back or kept under control.
- Fragrances should be avoided but if you must use them, do not let them be overpowering.

- Nails should be clean and well-manicured. They are seen constantly. Women – light polish only.
- Makeup should be light and professional.
- Mustaches and beards are still off-putting in some industries. If you can't live without them, make sure they are neatly trimmed at all times.
- Use deodorant.
- Keep a toothbrush and toothpaste at the office/fire house.
- Men – keep an electric razor for that five o'clock shadow.

Hot Tip: Look in the mirror before you leave. Is your appearance sending the right message?

Chapter in Review

Keep your look professional at all times. Ask if you are not sure what the appropriate dress is for the meeting or business social event.

Buy the most expensive clothes and accessories that you can afford. Don't mix your looks – high quality suit with bargain basement shoes.

Personal hygiene matters. It shows respect for others and for your job. Do not let sloppiness in your appearance reflect on you or your department.

WATCH, ASSESS, REACT

This chapter, while short, has three of the most important tips to help you navigate change in two areas. One – you are moving into a management position within the fire service. Or two – you are already in a management role and now your responsibilities have you working with individuals in the government or private sectors. It can be overwhelming when our new job responsibilities include working with organizations whose cultures are different than the fire service and building relationships that are not based on the comradery of the fire service family. You may be dealing with individuals that have no concept of what it's like to work in an environment like the fire service.

Know and understand that you will make some mistakes. That's fine as long as you can admit you made a mistake and learn from it. Every new position or added responsibility opens the door for learning, growing, and building your career success.

Power of Observation

Observation is the act of noticing, perceiving, watching, and paying attention to see or learn something.

Again, whether you are newly promoted within the fire service or are now working with outside organizations for the first time, this is the one step I have seen so many people skip! They take on the new job/responsibility and start to make changes or make suggestions to change things before they even understand the "why" behind the way things are currently structured or done. This approach is one of the fastest ways to introduce conflict into a department or new working relationship.

Here are a few simple tips that can aid you in developing this highly valuable skill. Take the time to learn and understand how things are done or why an organization does things a certain way before you attempt to change them or judge others.

- Ask questions, lots of them. Find out the "why."
- Talk to the people who are doing the actual work. Understand why policies and procedures are in place.

- When you move into fire service management and now have direct reports always ask what would make their job easier or more efficient, what would they recommend and why.
- If you have never done a subordinate's job try doing the task yourself to better understand the process.
- Keep an open mind – things may not need to be changed just tweaked a bit.
- If you do have a better way or an idea, share it with others and see if it is well-received and viable. Also, be open to change your original thoughts based on feedback you receive.

Hot Tip: Don't change things unless you absolutely understand how your suggested change will impact the employees and the department's policies and procedures.

As the "new kid on the block" come in softly and confidently. **Watch** what is currently being done, **Assess** the current process, what works and what doesn't, then **React** to the information you have learned. Allow your powers to observe to serve you so when you do move forward to make or suggest a change you have all the information you need and can show why the change is a good business decision for both the department and the company.

Culture Clash

Part of observation is listening to spoken and unspoken words. In the Communication chapter we'll concentrate on the spoken word. For now, I'd like to focus on the tone of voice of the messages and the body language signals that are being sent between people. A lot can be learned about the culture and the environment in which you work just by tuning in.

Unspoken words are between individuals that know each other well or have worked together for a long time. They can be communicated in someone's behavior or reaction to situations, their tone of voice, and body language. This type of communication can be positive or negative; it can be generational, peer, or hierarchy based. Learn the language of the unspoken word.

As with words, unspoken rules are important to learn and understand. Rules are the customary or normal conduct or practices within the department or company. Through your power of observation you should be able to tell what is the accepted policy or practice. Unspoken rule examples can be as simple as lunch or afternoon breaks. Following the rules is crucial to your co-workers acceptance and perception of you as a team player.

Know the rules, follow the rules and don't make up your own rules!

Hot Tip: Think sports - rules add structure, equalize the playing field, and help to build cohesive teams. The unspoken, unwritten rules are as important as the written policy rules.

Mining a Mentor
(find, approach, value)

Mentors are the unsung heroes in our career advancement and success. They come into our lives in many ways and types. My best mentors were my direct supervisors or other experienced managers I worked with throughout my career. They took me under their wing, showed me the ropes, answered my questions, and made time to talk to me when I was facing a difficult situation. They helped me to grow up, take on more responsibility, and were the best advocates for my career advancement. That's why you need to find and develop the relationships that will bring mentors into your circle of influence.

Important aspects about being the mentee (that would be you) – you need to be open to constructive criticism, be open-minded to change, be able to admit when you are wrong, and be able to ask for help when you need it. Asking for help is not a sign of weakness it's a sign of strength!

Information on mentors and mentees can be found in books, blogs, articles, web sites, even twitter. I pulled the information below from some of these resources that will help explain the mentor – mentee relationship.

Hot Tip: There is a difference between a Mentor, a Coach, and a Consultant. When starting out in a new position or gaining added responsibilities look for some great Mentors.

In the book *The Connectors* by Maribeth Kuzmeski there is a chapter titled: Find a Mentor – The Influence that Leads, Motivates and Holds You Accountable. The chapter begins with a quote from Tom Pace that I believe defines the "why" of the importance of finding a mentor, especially in the early stages of your career.

"You need mentors in your life to take you to the places you want to go!!! Why do you need mentors? Well it's simple. Mentors cause you to change, or stretch yourself to new limits not known before. They also give you a larger vision for your life than you can see for yourself."

The relationship between the mentor and mentee is usually one of an older more experienced person advising and helping a less experienced and often younger person in their career growth.

When you decide to start a mentor-mentee relationship, think of it in two steps: what do you as the mentee want to gain and accomplish and what do you want in a mentor.

Mentee Checklist

- Why do you want a mentor?
- What are your goals (new skills, understanding of business, etc.)? List them in order of priority.
- How can a mentor help you achieve your goals?
- How much time are you willing to commit to working with a mentor? Once a week, monthly, quarterly?

- Will you communicate face-to-face, by phone, by email or a combination?
- Can you be flexible as connecting will be based on your mentor's schedule?
- Are you prepared to keep commitments you make with a mentor?
- How will you track your goal achievements?
- Will you maintain your focus and enthusiasm towards this process and relationship building?
- Are you open to feedback and suggestions for improvement?

Mentor Qualities Checklist

- Does this person have the skills and experience you are looking for?
- Will this person have time in their schedule to work with you?
- Is this someone you will be comfortable talking to and sharing your ideas and areas of growth?
- Do you like this person?
- Do you believe this person is a good listener and has the desire to take on a mentee?
- Do you have trust in this person?
- Will this person be able to consistently challenge you?
- Will this person encourage you and provide the guidance you need to achieve your goals?

- Is this person respected within the organization?

How to Find a Mentor

Organizations – Through a professional or trade organization you may be able to find someone who meets your qualifications and is willing to become your mentor. If you do not belong to such a group you might consider joining one for several reasons: to find a mentor, to network, to take advantage of educational sessions. Professional organizations are particularly important if your field or position requires continuing education units to maintain your degree or certification.

Referrals – Is there someone at work that you admire, respect, and has made an impact with their insight and perceptiveness? It could be someone higher up in your department or division, perhaps someone from a different area of the fire service, or it could be an individual who isn't currently an executive but has lots of experience. Is there someone from outside the fire service that a friend or family member could recommend?

Here are some additional articles you might find helpful on mentoring:

Inc. Magazine on-line: *How to Find a Business Mentor*. http://www.inc.com/guides/how-to-find-a-business-mentor.html

Other websites:

http://www.topsuccesssite.com

www.leadershipdevelopmentservices.com

Books by Lois Zachary with Lory A. Fischler include *The Mentee's Guide, The Mentor's Guide,* and *Creating a Mentoring Culture.*

Chapter in Review

Power of Observation – Allow your powers to observe serve you so when you do move forward to make a change or suggest a change, you have all the information you need and can show why the change is a good business decision for both the department and the fire service.

Observe your work community – the people and the physical environment. Learn the spoken and unspoken rules. Make your transition softly, confidently, and successfully. You'll have the power to do so.

Mentoring is a professional relationship in which an experienced person (mentor) helps the mentee in developing skills and knowledge that will improve the mentee's professional and personal growth. Find a mentor or just be open to the idea that many of the experienced leaders you work with can be that "unsung hero" to you.

R.E.S.P.E.C.T.

When I talk to people about what "respect" means in the workplace I get a wide range of comments, definitions, and head shaking. So it's clear to me that a chapter on the subject is valuable. The challenge is how to make a truly complex subject simple.

Some of you may have heard the song "Respect," the 1967 hit and signature song for R&B singer Aretha Franklin. It was my inspiration for this acronym that helps define respect. Each word begins with a definition taken from Random House Webster's College Dictionary, 1991. You may think of other words that work for you and that's great. What does respect mean to you?

Receptive – "having the quality of receiving, taking in or admitting 2) able or quick to receive knowledge, ideas, etc. 3) willing or inclined to receive suggestions, offers, etc."

When you are receptive you pay attention to the world around you, listen to and engage with co-workers, union officials, and government or association personnel, and keep an open mind. Sometimes we think we are right and let our ego get in the way. As a human resource manager once said "lose the attitude" and become a receptive person.

Ethics – "a system or set of moral principles 2) the rules of conduct recognized in respect to a particular class of human actions or governing a particular group, culture, etc.: *medical ethics* 3) the branch of philosophy dealing with values relating to human conduct with respect to rightness and wrongness of actions and the goodness and badness of motives and ends 4) moral principles as of an individual: *His ethics forbade betrayal of a confidence.*"

What exactly is a set of moral principles? Most companies have an ethics statement about how they conduct business. The example I use with my students, as it relates to the Hospitality Industry, has to do with a FAM Trip (familiarization trip/hosted buyer event).

A hotel or a city invites meeting managers to visit and become familiar with their site or city in the hopes that these individuals will bring business. These excursions are usually paid for by the hotel or city. A question of ethics arises if you accept an invitation knowing that your company will not plan an event in that location. You only go because you want a free weekend away. Doing so is considered unethical in the Hospitality Industry. A FAM Trip is not a mini-vacation; it is a business trip.

I've had students ask me, "What if maybe someday in the future we might go to that location, can I still go?" If you will not be planning an event at the location within the next 12 months then you don't go. Ethics and ethical behavior are black and white and not shades of gray.

It's important that you know your department's code of ethics and rules. As you begin working with other organizations that may function on a different code, you might find yourself in an uncomfortable position. If this comes up and you aren't sure what the ethical response would be as a representative of the fire service, ask your supervisor or someone in a leadership role who can help.

<u>S</u>elf-control – "restraint of oneself or one's actions, feelings, etc."

Before getting offended or being indignant about a person's behavior or communication style, give them the benefit of the doubt. Many times a person is not even aware they are doing "something wrong" in the eyes of others. Based on where they stand their behavior probably makes perfect sense.

Think before you speak and react. Remember, outside the fire service it's a different world in acceptable business behaviors and interactions.

Polite – "showing good manners toward others, as in behavior or speech; courteous: *a polite reply* 2) refined or cultured: *polite society* 3) of a refined or elegant kind: *polite learning.*"

Small courtesies go a long way. Acknowledge and greet others especially if you do not know them; a simple "good morning" or "hello" lets the person know you are aware of them. We all like to be recognized! Try adding the words "please" and "thank-you" to your requests to others. Use the person's name. It makes them feel like they matter. Hold the door open for someone. Smile. I bet you could list ten more things you could do to be more polite in any work or social activity.

<u>Esteem</u> – "to regard highly or favorably; regard with respect or admiration . . . 4)

favorable opinion or judgment; respect or regard: *to hold a person in esteem*."

I like this term. It brings to mind a select group of individuals with whom I had the privilege to work. These were the people who taught me and were great role models and mentors. I held them in "high esteem."

Who do you hold in high esteem: a captain or lieutenant, training instructor, manager, spiritual leader, or a relative? These are the people who helped you to grow. Look around, who are the individuals that can help you now to develop in your career? Most likely you already respect them and hold them in esteem.

Consider – "to think carefully about, esp. in order to make a decision; contemplate; ponder 2) to regard with respect or thoughtfulness; show consideration for; to consider other people's feelings."

This is the next step after Receptive. You have listened and taken in the information, had an open dialogue, asked questions and have a good understanding. You are now in the consider stage. It's time to think carefully before you respond. You always want to respond thoughtfully and to consider the feeling of others.

<u>Thanks</u> – "to express gratitude or appreciation to 2) a grateful feeling or acknowledgment of a kindness, favor or the like, expressed by words or otherwise."

This is such an important word that expresses so much feeling. Sometimes I think it's a lost art! It's so easy to say "thank you" to others that have helped you in some way.

Say "thank you" to someone when they: hold a door for you, get you the information you asked for, bring you lunch or a coffee, support you in a meeting, or return your phone call. The list could go on and on. What are some other reasons to extend a thank you?

A simple thank you can be a verbal response, an email, phone call, or a handwritten note.

Make it a practice to say thank you as part of your daily routine; it goes a long way and people appreciate it more than you will ever know.

Hot Tip: These behaviors govern how we act, communicate, and interact with others every day. They are how good business is done and relationships are built.

Four Generations in the Workplace
Why R.E.S.P.E.C.T. Makes It Work

Men resemble their times more so than their fathers.
> Ibn Khaldun, 1332-1406, Arab Philosopher and
> Demographer

R.E.S.P.E.C.T. What does it have to do with business today? Plenty. One of the most frequent complaints I hear when consulting with businesses is that there is not enough civility and respect in the workplace. But work is exactly where we need to practice it.

The problem is, each of us has a different idea of what R.E.S.P.E.C.T. looks like. We have our own ideas of acceptable behavior based on our age, up-bringing, education, and other factors that shaped us. With up to four generations in the work place today, it's easy to see how conflict and misunderstandings occur.

One of the biggest challenges facing today's management is blending the four generations into cohesive working teams. It's important to recognize that differences exist between the generations and it's those differences that can help explain the behaviors and perceptions you might see from others. That's why this subject is under the R.E.S.P.E.C.T. chapter.

Respect each generation and find common ground in order to learn from one another.

There are many books and resources on generational differences. I encourage you to read some of them to get a better understanding of each generation so that you can be effective in the workplace. In this chapter I hope to plant a few seeds of curiosity and provide a high level look at what shapes us. Keep in mind these are generalities, not hard and fast rules that apply to every person in each generation.

Things to consider in a blended generational work environment:

- Start by being aware that differences exist and don't jump to conclusions about another's behavior.
- Dates for each generation are not set in stone; depending on the source the years can vary slightly.
- Each generation has shared social and historical experiences. Current events, social and economic trends, pop culture, (music/fashion/movies) etc.
- These shared social and historical experiences shape values both at work and in private life.

- Accept how all of the above impacts expectations and behaviors in the workplace.
- Language. Each generation has its own lexicon and slang. It's easy to leave someone out of the conversation when we use it. What should you do? Ask the person to explain what they meant before you make a judgment. This allows for sharing experiences and opens both of you to understanding one another.

Multi-Generational Challenges:

- Communication preferences – ask how a person would like to receive communication – not everyone likes a text message.
- Definition of work "day" – Gen Z, the Millennials, and Gen X generations prefer flexible hours and days although their motivation is different. Millennials relate work to a "life style" they are living. This may translate in "I don't want to work overtime. I've already put in my hours." Gen X's lifestyle has also moved from the structured 8 to 5 workday but their movement is due to caring for aging parents.

- Work assignments – some respond better to a planned way of doing things, others like the freedom to approach the tasks in a manner they feel suits their working style.
- Promotional opportunities – making sure everyone understands what skills and qualifications are required in order to be considered for promotion. Seniority level or length of employment doesn't always mean you get promoted.
- Division policies – execution and implementation of policies and procedures especially if one is not in agreement with the change. Some individuals will adapt while others will challenge the process.

Employees of all generations view work as an extension of themselves:

- Seek personal fulfillment and satisfaction from their job.
- Want compensation that is fair in the current marketplace.
- Highest indicator of job satisfaction within all generations is feeling valued for the work they perform.

- The workplace culture cultivated by the organization and its managers directly relates to the overall job satisfaction felt by all employees. A majority (over 70%) of employees prefer a work environment where they feel appreciated, supported, and recognized.
- Career development is a high priority among all generations; only half of them feel their current employer does a good job of supporting this interest.
- Offering a flexible work schedule to accommodate individuals goes a long way with employees in each generation.
- Seven out of ten workers would like to set their own work hours, as long as the work that needs to get done is done at the highest quality and on time. This may not seem related to the fire service culture however based on the desires of the younger generations it may create challenges for supervisors as they build their teams due to higher rates of turn-over.

Hot Tip: Keep in mind that we all can make changes in our behavior to get along better with others. But change isn't always easy.

Chapter in Review

As you go about changing your awareness and your behavior to create a more productive and harmonious work environment, remember it takes time. For example, to start a new behavior – you must practice that behavior for about 66 days to begin a new pattern.

It takes 100 days for the pattern to become automatic – continue to practice the new behavior to really make it stick.

Make a point to understand the different generations in your workplace. Use R.E.S.P.E.C.T. to develop better working relationships and to promote a more profitable and friendly business environment.

Hot Tip: Always be considerate. Always be respectful. Always be polite.

COMMUNICATIONS

"The newest computer can merely compound, at speed, the oldest problem in the relations between human beings, and in the end the communicator will be confronted with the old problem, of what to say and how to say it." Edward R. Murrow, American news broadcaster

The need to effectively communicate in the workplace has not changed in the 21st century. What has changed is the cultural and technological diversity.

Age – currently there are four generations in the workforce, each with their own preferences and comfort in communication styles.

Nationalities – we are a multi-cultural nation and that brings a wide range of customs, languages, and work ethics to the workplace.

Technologies – from email to twitter the challenge is how best to use these tools.

Working environments – is it a building you go to, a home office, or a virtual office?

International companies – customs, time zones, written word, language differences, and difficulty in building relationships all contribute to the communications challenge.

As we talk about communication I'd like you to visualize a bicycle wheel and you are the center of it. Every spoke that fans out from you represents individuals in other fire service departments and divisions, mangers, team members, government, union, or private businesses. You may need to communicate with all of these people in order to complete your job responsibilities. You might engage with them daily, weekly, monthly or only yearly, but they are all vital to how your organization does business day-to-day and how you succeed at your job

Your challenge is to understand who you need to communicate with and why. Then, keeping the above diversities in mind, determine how best to communicate. Communication is hard work and it is a behavioral skill well worth learning.

There are two aspects of communication:

- Verbal – speaking and listening: face-to-face, phone, or voice mail.

- Written – words you write: paper, email, Twitter, Facebook, etc.

Verbal Communication

Google "verbal communication" and you will get over 9,670,000 hits! In the simplest of terms, verbal communication is your voice that makes sounds that are converted to words that convey a message to another person. This can be face-to-face, by phone, through voice mail, on Face Time, Skype, live video, or satellite conference, etc. Basically, anytime you are speaking and someone can hear your voice you are sending a verbal message.

Verbal messages can bring a range of challenges and communication breakdowns. Some of these are: bad choice of words, different points of view, misunderstood message, language difficulty, and poor communication skills. Even your social class, education level, or where you live can create misunderstanding when the other person doesn't interpret your message as you intended.

The delivery system (that's you) is what creates communication breakdowns. However, you can get your message across regardless of the circumstances. Even if you are angry, upset, or confused, effective communication is within your ability. Real communication starts with these two important principles:

1st A person's perception is their reality. How a person looks at a situation is how they are going to respond in that moment – that's what is real to them. You don't have to like it or agree with their response but you do have to accept it because that's what is true for that person.

2nd The situation (person, place, or thing) *does not* dictate your response. You and only you have the choice as to how you will respond. And your reaction, i.e. tone of voice, words and phrases used, and even your non-verbal body language, has an impact on the outcome of the situation at hand.

Hot Tip: Don't get confused between the words agree and accept. *Agree* is to be of one mind; harmonize in opinion or feeling. *Accept* is to accommodate or reconcile oneself to accept the situation. (Random House Webster College Dictionary)

Verbal communication has to do with politeness, respect, self-control, good manners and an open mind!

"Words are the most powerful drug used by mankind."
Rudyard Kipling, English Writer

Key points on what constitutes an effective verbal delivery system:

- Don't discount the power of your words. Always think before you speak – once the words are out, you can't get them back.
- Keep the volume of your voice moderate at all times, a loud voice can be annoying, intimidating, or threatening.
- Make sure you need to speak. Sometimes silence can be kinder and more considerate than words.
- Avoid going off on a tangent.
- Stop when you have made your point and let the other person speak.
- Never yell at anyone.
- You can be angry and still be civil – it's the words used and tone of voice.
- Never utter unkind words regarding a person's racial, national, sexual, or gender identity.
- Never use profanities – fastest way to offend someone.

- Never embarrass.

Don't say mean words or gossip about others – it can hurt their reputation and their feelings if the words get back to them. This can make you look untrustworthy, i.e. if you are willing to bad-mouth others then you're likely to bad-mouth me as well.

A good way to end this section on verbal communication is with these two great quotes:

"Two monologues do not make a dialogue."
Jeffrey L. Daly - American architect

"The ability to speak eloquently is not to be confused with having something to say."
Michael P. Hart, from Areia Gloris/Yes to Riches/Top 7 Communication Quotes

Learning to Listen

"If you just communicate you can get by. But if you skillfully communicate, you can work miracles."
Jim Rohn, American business philosopher and author

What is listening? Listening is the skill to correctly receive and understand verbal messages during the communication process. We use our ears to hear sounds that we translate into words. We use our mind to interpret the words to the message to what we think is being sent.

Why is listening important? Verbal messages can easily be misinterpreted. When this happens the sender of the message can become frustrated, irritated, or even angry.

Even more importantly, the speaker could walk away thinking you don't have the capability to understand what's been said or you simply don't care. Leaving that type of impression is not good for your reputation, particularly if the speaker is your boss, a senior executive or a government official. The end result is bad decisions may be made on information that was interpreted incorrectly. Excellent listening skills can prevent this type of mishap at work.

Remember, communication is never one-way. As a listener you are even more responsible than the speaker for ensuring communication occurs. Why? Well, the speaker can only communicate when you allow his or her words to get through. Otherwise, the speaker is merely making sounds, blah, blah, blah; there is no communication. True communication is about interaction and striving to understand.

How to be a better listener? The easiest approach is to always be receptive to the other person. In *Choosing Civility, The Twenty-five Rules of Considerate Conduct*, P. M. Forni defines being receptive as:

"Receptivity is the willingness to listen to the other person and consider what he's saying. It's the willingness to take in (receive) what the other person knows, believes, thinks, and feels. It's the willingness to pay attention, to concentrate, to weigh, to evaluate, to mull over.

The receptive person is willing to give the other person a chance to get through; he's willing to cooperate in the communication process. This doesn't mean he agrees with what he hears; it only means he will consider it."

Practice these few tips until they become part of your everyday behavior and style.

- Plan to listen – listen with no other purpose than to listen. Keep an open mind – listen carefully. Sometimes this is not easy if we have already made up our mind on what we believe the outcome should be. The listening with an open mind approach allows you to ask better questions, get information that you may not have been aware of and move you toward better decision making. You may gain valuable information. You might also gain a better understanding of the other person's point of view.

- Indicate you are listening, say something like, "I wasn't aware of that" or "That's interesting, tell me more."
- Answer questions raised by the other person. Don't be afraid to answer and share information unless it's confidential. If you don't have the answer let them know you will get it and get back to them in a reasonable timeframe. Then keep your commitment.
- Ask questions to clarify what the other person means if you are unsure. Be clear on where you are confused or unsure of their meaning. Don't be vague!
- Use the open-ended question technique. Don't ask a question that can be responded to with either a yes or no.
- No need to rush to agree or disagree; it's better to show you understand the issues at hand. This helps the person to know you have listened. An easy way to get clarification is to use the technique

of restating what you believe the other person has said. An example might be "Mary, let me see if I understood what you meant regarding final deadlines. The project needs to be 100% complete by the last Friday of this month."

Hot Tip: *"Much of the conflict in our lives can be explained by one simple but unhappy fact: we don't really listen to each other."* **Michael P. Nichols,** author of *The Lost Art of Listening*

Telephone Etiquette

Today we almost always expect to get the person's voice mail and not the actual person when we call. If we do get a live person it can throw us off. In either case, take the time to prepare for your call. It will save you time and promote good relationships.

Placing the Call

- Prepare by writing down any specific questions and topics to cover – this will help keep the conversation on track and on time.

- Have available facts, figures and documentation needed – saves time and you look organized and prepared.
- Blank paper/notebook and pen for taking notes.
- When using a computer to take notes let the other person know that you will be typing so the sound of the keys will not be distracting or give the impression you are working on something other than the conversation.
- Calendar to set follow-up dates – not to overbook.
- Always identify yourself with your first and last name and fire service affiliation. This reinforces name recognition.
- Quickly explain reason for call.
- When it's an unscheduled call always ask if it's a good time to talk. If not, ask when would be a better time to call back.
- After the call send a recap email – highlight key points/decisions made, follow-up actions/who is responsible and date and time of next meeting or call.

Wrong Numbers

- Don't hang up say, "I'm sorry. I must have dialed the wrong number."
- Give the number you called so you don't make the same mistake twice.

Put on Hold

- If you are pressed for time, tell the gatekeeper you would like to leave a message or be transferred to voice mail.
- If on hold more than three minutes it is okay to hang up and call back later.
- Be courteous when you do connect with the person, politely say you couldn't hold – no explanation is required.

Speaker Phone/Conference Call

- Immediately tell the person(s) on the other end that you are using a speaker-phone and ask if that is "ok."
- Have each person introduce themselves so all on the call can identify names and voices.
- When someone joins the conversation after the initial introductions, be sure to politely stop the conversation and intro-duce the new person. It shows good

manners to be sure everyone knows who is on the call at all times.

- Use a person's name during the call – "James, Nancy has a question for you." or "This is Michael and I would like to comment on . . . . "
- Close the office door during the call. If you don't have an office see if a meeting room is available that does have a door.
- When on a conference call, remember that your background noise can be disruptive to others so mute your phone when you are not speaking.

Phone Call Faux Pas – Common Mistakes to Avoid

- Don't do other things at your desk while talking like typing or shuffling papers. Concentrate on the conversation and listen; when you are doing other things you are not listening.
- No eating while on the phone.
- Turn off music.
- Never chew gum while talking on the phone.
- Don't sneeze, blow your nose, or cough directly into the receiver. Either excuse yourself for a moment or turn your head away.

- Gently put the receiver down on the desk if you have to during the conversation.
- Be careful not to address a person by their first name in sentence after sentence; it sounds insincere and patronizing.
- Don't answer a phone call when in a meeting or place a person on hold to take another call during a conversation.
- Never place someone on hold without permission.
- Don't stalk a person while they are on the phone – come back later.

Answering Business Calls

- Always try to answer the phone. Incoming calls answered by a person instead of a machine make a good impression for both you and the organization.
- Forget personal problems. Your voice should sound pleasant and calm when you answer the phone. Remember you are speaking as a representative of the company, not yourself.
- Answer the phone promptly – by the third ring if possible.

- Answer with something like "This is Michael Guerra speaking, how may I help you?"
- If you are really busy or in the middle of a project don't take the call, or if you do, let the person know you can't talk now and set up a time that works for both of you.

Returning Calls

- Return calls as soon as possible. Twenty-four hours is as long as a call can go unreturned without violating the precepts of good manners.

Leaving a Voice Mail Message

Treat recording devises with good manners. A message left in an upbeat tone of voice gives the recipient of the call confidence in both you and your company; an irritated tone does quite the opposite.

- Don't speak too fast – slow down especially when you leave the return phone number.
- Always leave your name, organization name, and return phone number twice

during the message. Usually once at the beginning and again at the end.

- Give enough information in the message. Provide the reason for the call; keep it short and to the point. No rambling messages!
- Assume the person will answer and be prepared to have a conversation.
- Don't fill up another person's voice mailbox; one message a day is enough.
- Never use a voice system to avoid a difficult conversation.

Your Recorded Voice Mail Greeting

- Keep the tone of your voice upbeat.
- Speak naturally and with an even pace – not too fast or too slow.
- Keep your message simple and short. "Hi, this is Sally Smith. Sorry I'm unable to take your call at this time. Please leave a brief message and your phone number and I will get back to you as soon as I am able."
- You may want to update your message daily if you are out of the office and give a date when the call will be returned.
- When on vacation or extended time out of the office leave the name and phone

number of someone they can contact during your absence. Also, leave your return date to the office or when they can expect a return call from you.

Cell Phone

- Put it away and on silent mode when in meetings or face-to-face conversations.
- It is rude and *not okay* to read/respond to an email, text or to IM someone while you are face-to-face with another person or in a meeting.
- If you must look at or answer your phone excuse yourself for a few minutes so you don't send the message that the person(s) you are with is not as important as the email, text, or call.
- When away from your desk don't use the phone if it will bother people around you – move to a place that is private.
- Absolutely never say anything confidential, personal, or private if others can overhear you. Instead arrange to call the person back at a later time.
- Speak quietly – people don't want to hear your conversation; it's distracting.

- Don't overdo it. Brief conversation isn't likely to disturb anyone, but an hour of continuous use may drive those around you crazy.
- Be safe when using the cell phone. That means while driving or walking. Don't stop suddenly to write, text, or answer the phone. Your inattention or lack of awareness to your surroundings and environment could negatively impact another person.

> **Hot Tip:** Know your division's policy regarding the use of cell phones especially if used in a vehicle while on the job.

Writing Protocols

You don't write because you want to say something; you write because you've got something to say.
F. Scott Fitzgerald, American author

This quote from Barbara Pachter, Business Communications Consultant and etiquette expert, says it all. *"Words have power, and written words have lasting power.*" The way we communicate has changed dramatically in the last decade thanks to email, voice mail and social networking sites. In the business world one thing has not changed – the importance of our words and the need to write them clearly and effectively.

When you put your thoughts in writing, it's a concrete representation of your command of the language, your writing skills and, most importantly, your professionalism. Your writing says a lot about you and the fire service you represent.

Good writing must meet the four C's. Ask yourself, is it:

- **Correct?** Does it accurately describe the situation?
- **Clear?** Have you said what you intended to say?
- **Coherent?** Will the reader understand?
- **Clean?** Are there any grammatical mistakes or misspelled words?

Key points to successful letter writing are keeping it straightforward and uncomplicated.

- Organize your thoughts before you start, always write a rough draft.
- Write a good opening sentence. If you don't capture their attention, they may not read the rest.
- Use the proper title of the person with whom you are corresponding. It can be insulting to the person if their title is incorrect.
- Address them by their full name, unless your relationship with them warrants more familiarity.
- Verify that their name is spelled correctly. Few things are more annoying than seeing your name misspelled.
- Write in the first person unless the letter is representing the company as a whole.
- Be natural; write in complete sentences, leave out interjections and excessive use of pronouns.
- Keep it short; write only what will get the message across, include important information. Eliminate extra words.
- Use bullet points when possible.
- Avoid clichés and buzzwords; use everyday language.

- Avoid technical jargon and specialized language unless you are certain the reader is familiar with the field.
- Proofread. Read and reread for spelling, grammar, and punctuation errors. Never rely totally on the computer's spelling and grammar checks. "Pleas sea hour lay test add" will pass as will "Please see our latest ad."
- Read it out loud to someone or yourself – reading out loud will help to catch awkward or cumbersome phrasing and omitted words.
- Use humor thoughtfully and selectively. What is funny to one can be offensive to another.
- Avoid negative phasing – "You forgot to attach the waiver." vs. "Please remember to include the waiver in the future."
- Make sure you communicate correctly for the intended reader. A letter to a colleague would be written differently than one to a senior executive.

Hot Tip: Words are things. Each word conveys a specific meaning. The difference in words can be subtle – choose them wisely.

Emails, Text and IM Messages

RU, LOL, TTYL. It looks like a foreign language or a secret code, but it's a new form of writing. Today our need for speed – fast internet, downloads, phone connections – has given way to a fast way to write, text, or IM a person. This may be acceptable on a social level, but it is not acceptable in the business world. The person receiving the message needs to comprehend what you are saying and not everyone understands this newer form of writing.

The rules of good writing apply to email, text and IM messages as well. Whether you are using a cell phone, tablet, laptop or desk top, remember to start with the basics and don't use the new word shortcuts.

- Understand the rules of writing still apply.
- Follow division guidelines on appropriate use of email.
- Don't contribute to email overload. You should respect other people's "electronic space."
- Appropriate use of Cc's and Bcc's – who really needs to see the message?

- Not all Cc's on an email need to see the reply – example if it's just a "Thanks" only the person sending the email needs to be on the reply. Biggest complaint with email is unnecessary emails due to "reply all" when it's not needed. Think who really needs to read and know the information in the email.
- Don't give out someone's email address without permission.
- Don't assume that everybody wants to correspond by email, text or IM. Always ask the person what is their preferred way to communicate.
- Check your email regularly.
- Respond in a reasonable amount of time – best practice is within 24 hours.
- Do not mark urgent, unless it is.
- Never forward unless you know it would be appropriate.
- Use the "out of office" auto reply.
- Use "return receipt" only if necessary.
- Keep messages short and simple.
- Use short paragraphs or bullet points.
- Always use appropriate business language; no slang, abbreviations or jokes.
- Always use the subject line.
- DON'T USE ALL CAP LETTERS – save them for emphasis.

- Don't use emoticon faces or special characters to express your mood, i.e. happy :), sad :(, etc. It is unprofessional.
- Don't' write anything about anyone that you would not say to that person.
- Proofread, proofread, and proofread before you hit the send key.
- Don't send a message containing any business information that should be kept confidential.
- Don't email when upset or angry; put it in the "drafts box" and come back to it in a few hours or the next day. You'll almost certainly make changes – remember, once you hit the send key you won't get it back so be sure the tone is professional and not offensive.
- Don't email for important thank-you notes.
- Salutations and closings should be used if it's a new email. Once in the "reply" process they are not technically required but nice.

Hot Tip: There is no privacy protection for emails at your job. Stop and think about the content before you hit send.

Chapter in Review

Verbal communication – any time you are speaking and someone can hear your voice you are sending a "verbal message." Make sure the message delivered is polite, respectful, controlled, has a pleasant tone, and positive words.

Learn to Listen – Remember it's the listener who communicates, not the speaker. Communication requires a dialogue; a back-and-forth conversation.

Telephone Etiquette – Proper phone protocols are essential to how you come across as a professional and how well you represent the fire service.

Writing Protocols – When you put your thoughts in writing, it's a concrete representation of your command of the language, your writing skills and, most importantly, your professionalism. Your writing says a lot about you and the fire service you represent.

MEETING MASTERY

It's easy to think you just have to show up at a meeting to make an impression – think again. As a spokesperson for the fire service and now being in a public forum, follow these simple business behaviors to earn respect and appreciation.

1. Arrive on time – sounds like common sense, but think about how many meetings you have attended where the group had to wait for someone. Or worse yet, stop the meeting in progress and have to recap for the late comer. It is rude and disrespectful to the other participants to arrive late and disrupt the meeting. It's a time waster!

2. Dress – always wear the appropriate fire service uniform for the type of meeting you are participating in. A "business casual" meeting in an office would reflect the fire service's more casual dress. On the other hand, a meeting with the Governor might require the official dress uniform. If you are unsure call the meeting organizer to find out who will be in attendance and the recommended dress code.

3. Introductions – if administrative personnel are present, always greet them and introduce yourself if you do not know them. People do not like to be ignored; be friendly and respectful. The same is true for each participant who is attending the meeting – greet the ones you know and be sure to introduce yourself and shake hands with those you do not know.

Hot Tip: Always stand when being introduced. The highest ranking person should initiate the handshake for newcomers to the meeting.

---

4. Be prepared – there is a reason for your participation in the meeting or you would not have been invited. Know the agenda in advance and come ready to contribute to the discussion. If you are unsure of what you are expected to contribute, call the meeting organizer or your supervisor and find out. You can't be prepared if you don't know what is expected of you. Remember never offer information or data unless you are sure it is correct and you can provide back-up documentation. Be an enthusiastic team player; listen to others and share information.

5. Turn off your phone – if expecting an "emergency" call, place your phone in silence mode and notify the meeting facilitator. If you get a call, leave the room to answer. Make sure to quietly close the door behind you. Understand when you look at your phone or emails during a meeting you are sending a very clear message that other things are more important than the meeting and its participants. Others do notice that you're not paying attention. *This is not okay.*

6. Note taking – If you use your laptop, tablet, or phone to take notes during the meeting, let the facilitator and others know. This way they won't think you're doing something else like responding to emails or posting to Facebook.

7. Pay attention – each person speaking deserves your attention. This means no playing with your pen, no doodling, no staring out the window, and yes, you guessed it, no messing with your phone (see point 5). All of these bad habits give the impression that you are not paying attention even if you are.

> **Hot Tip:** Don't interrupt another person while they are talking. It's rude and bad manners. Let the person complete their thoughts before you make your comments.

8. Side-bar conversations – keep to a minimum or not at all. It's distracting and rude. Covering your mouth while taking to the person next to you does not stop others from seeing and maybe hearing your conversation. You may miss something and have to ask to have it repeated. This is a waste of other people's time.

9. Other time wasters – If a topic or point has already been discussed don't bring it up again unless you have something important to add. And don't add a new topic of discussion to the agenda unless approved by the meeting organizer.

10. Clean up – Before you leave the meeting pick up your trash and toss it out. It's not okay to let others clean up your mess.

11. Meetings in a restaurant – see the chapter on Dining Skills.

> **Hot Tip:** Maintain a professional image during the meeting: have good posture, no slouching, no grooming yourself – biting your nails, putting on lipstick, combing your hair, etc. It is inappropriate behavior; people will notice and remember.

Chapter in Review

Meetings are an important part of everyday business. How you show up and your participation are key to career success. The eleven points in this chapter may seem like common sense however when people don't follow them they become the top frustrations and pet peeves for meeting attendees. Avoid these common mistakes and faux pas.

Meeting manners count. Make sure you learn them, practice them, and become a true meeting professional.

EXTINGUISH PUBLIC SPEAKING FEAR

Most people don't like to stand up in front of an audience to give a talk or presentation. Some are even uncomfortable presenting their information in community business meetings, especially in front of union leaders or elected officials. Stage fright is the number one obstacle in giving a presentation. People feel nervous, get "butterflies" in their stomach, and feel like they can't remember what to say. But take heart, if you have stage fright you are in the majority.

The most important thing you can do is to simply acknowledge that giving a presentation is an uncomfortable task for you. Notice I didn't say a weakness; it's simply an area where you need some help in developing the skills that give you the confidence to talk before a group. The uneasiness you feel just before you talk is really just adrenaline, a natural "energy boost!" Any top athlete or performer has this same adrenaline energy rush that helps them to perform their best.

The first step in improving your presentation skills is to stop thinking of it as a negative task or experience. Think of it as your chance to stand out and represent the fire service in the best light. Or remind yourself that someone has confidence in your ability and you should be proud that you were asked to present.

The three P's of public speaking are skills and behaviors you can learn that will make presenting to an audience easier. Master these soft skills and the confidence and polish required to give a professional presentation will be yours.

First P – Preparation

Who are you speaking to? There could be a difference between who is in the audience and who the target group is you want to reach. In composing your talk, it's important to focus on who will be in the room. Know your audience!

Organize the presentation properly

There are three clear-cut parts to any presentation: the introduction, the main body and the conclusion. Make sure you have all three or your presentation will not be cohesive.

1. **Introduction should explain the purpose** – It's important to let the audience know during the introduction the reason for the talk and what they will learn, such as being aware of the most frequent causes of residential fires.

   Also make sure you grab their attention in the beginning. Start with a related story, quote an expert or statistic, or ask a question like, "Did you know that in 2015, according to the U.S Fire Administration, 50.8% of residential building fires were caused by cooking?"

   Note: Be very careful with humor. Keep it refined. If you have doubts then don't use it. Humor can add to any talk; just make sure it works.

2. **Main body** – There should only be three to five main points. That's about as much as the audience can absorb and process. Back up each of the points with stories, pictures, facts or details.

3. **Conclusion** – Make sure the close is effective. Briefly recap the main points and end on a positive note or a call to action. In the speaking industry we have what we call "The Phrase that

Pays." To help anchor your message use something like, "If nothing else, please remember . . . ." or "The question I leave you with is . . . ." or "I encourage you to . . . ."

Practice

"Practice makes perfect," so take the time to practice the presentation out loud and in front of a mirror. Ask someone, not a part of the fire service, to hear your presentation; they will let you know if it makes sense and flows nicely. Be open to their feedback.

> **Hot Tip:** The more times you practice the more comfortable and confident you will be with the delivery of the material.

Second P - Physical Considerations

1. Dress appropriately for the audience you are addressing. You want to be as comfortable as possible in your uniform.

2. Arrive early to check room set-up, where the stage is located, size of room, where will you be seated before your introduction, etc.

3. Meet with audio visual technician to check all the equipment, do a sound check if using a microphone and double check internet connection if using it during the presentation.

4. Keep Power Point slides simple - use a title and three bullet points per slide and go easy with the graphics.

5. Be sure to have room temperature water on stage, use a flat bottom glass.

6. Take your name badge off while speaking.

Third P – Performance

Connect with your audience rather than merely speaking to your audience.

1. Arriving early also gives you the opportunity to walk around and meet people. You may hear a story or comment that relates to your topic that you can include during your talk.

2. Posture is key. Stand with your legs 4-6 inches apart to help with weight distribution and make sure to keep your shoulders back.

3. Make eye contact with one person per thought; move eyes around the room. This projects a sense of confidence and connection.

It takes a bit of practice however it's a powerful way to connect.

4. Watch your hand gestures. Never point a finger at the audience. Instead use an open hand with your palm up.

5. Vary the volume rate and pitch of your voice.

6. Include many "you-focused" phrases rather than "I-focused" phrases.

7. Every 5 – 10 minutes change your pace or your place on stage. Make a mark where you should do this in your notes.

8. Don't confuse or overwhelm with statistics. Don't use acronyms that relate to the fire service that the audience may not understand.

9. Following the conclusion take questions if appropriate. Always repeat the question before you give you answer to ensure everyone has heard what is being asked.

10. Be sure to thank those that should be given recognition.

Chapter in Review

A professional presentation can be a truly scary event for many people. Chances are you will be asked, at some point in your career, to give a presentation. Now is a great time to begin working on your presentation skills. The three P's can help you get started. Toastmasters International may be a good resource for you if you need practice. Their meetings are learn-by-doing workshops in which participants hone their speaking and leadership skills in a no-pressure atmosphere.

You can find a chapter near you at:
http://www.toastmasters.org/

For a Public Speaking workshop designed for your association or division you may contact Marla directly at: marla@actwelldowell.com

DINING SKILLS FOR THE SAVVY PROFESSIONAL

"The world was my oyster but I used the wrong fork."
Oscar Wilde

Every culture has their style or acceptable way of eating a meal. The firehouse has its own customary ways as well. I'm often told by fire fighters, who have taken my dining seminar that it would be quite the "eye opener" for them! On the flip side they often comment who knew there were so many protocols attached to eating a business meal.

It's a fact of life that business happens over meals. For someone going from the firehouse to a formal fundraising dinner or lunch with the Mayor, the meal takes on a different meaning in its purpose, your reason for being there, and the need to have polished table manners.

Knowing the dining rules no one ever told you will help you make a positive impression and project confidence. The key reason you want to have excellent dining skills is they allow you to focus on the conversation, the reason you were invited, and not worry about which fork you should use or where the bread plate is. It's about being comfortable when you sit down for a business meeting that includes a meal.

1 – You Said "Yes" – Now What?

As the invitee, it's your obligation to be an appreciative, positive, and accommodating guest. The following tips will give you the savvy social skills to that reflect your professionalism as well as that of the fire service.

- Arrive early, 10 to 15 minutes prior to the meeting time is acceptable. There is an old saying, "If you show up on time you are late!"
- Great your host before acknowledging others. If the host is in conversation with another person wait if possible for their conversation to end before you take your seat.

- Don't act shy. Introduce yourself to others you don't know and acknowledge those you do.
- Remember to smile and look other guests in the eye, especially during introductions and handshakes.
- Be careful not to talk only with people you know. Mingle with all the guests.
- Write a thank-you note within twenty-four hours.

This last point is crucial. A handwritten card will make you look world class! A thank-you note is simple to write. It can be as brief as three sentences that include a greeting, something positive about the person and/or event, and reference to a follow-up meeting or call if one was agreed upon. Then add your signature closing and you're done! Here's an example of a simple thank-you.

Dear Joseph,

Thank you for the invitation to speak at your association's June meeting. Your members made me feel welcomed and were really receptive to my talk. I look forward to seeing you next week at the city council meeting.

Sincerely,
Tom Smith

> **Really Hot Tip:** Have the card envelope already written out and stamped. Then after the meal write your short note and drop it in the mail.

An email or text message thank-you is acceptable but it is not as impactful or as professional as the old-fashioned, handwritten note.

> **Hot Tip:** RSVP means reply if you please. Or in French, Répondez s'il vous plait. Accept or decline within 48 hours. Should you need to cancel, do it personally. Canceling by phone is best rather than an email or text message.

Taking Your Seat and Napkin Etiquette

- Wait for your host to indicate where you will sit if you are unsure.
- Approach the chair on its right side, pull it away from the table if necessary, and enter it from your left side. When the meal is over, or you are leaving the table for a short time, push the chair back from the table, stand and exit from the right side and push the chair under the table.

- Once your host picks up her napkin, pick up your napkin quietly and fold it in half. Place fold close to your waist with the open end facing your knees. Open the napkin on your lap not in the air.
- When you are leaving the table, fold your napkin and put it on the seat of your chair. This gesture tells others, "I will be back."
- When done with the meal and leaving the table place your unfolded napkin to the left of the plate.

Note: At business meals, women should seat themselves and never expect a man to seat them. However, if a man does offers to seat you, accept with a polite *"thank you."*

At the Table

- If you are at a restaurant order from the middle of the price range on the menu — not the most or least expensive items.
- Posture is important it shows you are comfortable and confident. Sit straight with your back to the back of the chair and have both feet flat on the floor. Don't slouch or be too rigid.

- Elbows keep close to your side and don't place forearms or elbows on the table.
- When not eating, rest your hands on your lap or from the wrist up on the table's edge.
- When leaving the table to take a phone call or restroom break say, "Excuse me." You don't need to inform the table where you are going.
- For a sudden sneeze, turn your head to your shoulder and cover mouth with your napkin or handkerchief – simply say "Please excuse me."
- Never use your napkin to wipe your nose.

Know Your Place (Settings that is)

Think of the letters "B-M-W." They stand for:

- Bread – your bread plate is on your left.
- Meal – the main, center plate of the place setting.
- Water or wine – your glasses will be on the right. That includes your coffee cup and saucer.

Navigating your place setting requires some attention. Practice these tips before your meeting occurs. You'll feel much more comfortable and confident during the meal.

In an American-style place setting:

- Forks are on the left of the place setting. The outer fork may be smaller as it is used for the salad course if it is served first.
- Use the utensils located farthest from the plate first. For example, the first fork you use will be in the left outermost position of the place setting.
- Once used, the part of the utensil that was in your mouth never touches the table again. It must go on your plate, though the handle can extend off the plate. If it is a knife, the blade points downward with cutting edge facing the center of the plate.

American

Here is what the setting would look like with all the possible pieces.

Place Setting Map

2 - During the Meal

Preparing to Eat

- Eat with one hand and rest the other hand on the table at the wrist. Years ago, the rule was to keep one hand in your lap, but that is no longer regarded as mannerly.
- Taste your food before seasoning it with salt and pepper. If you must add salt, don't just grab it. If it is too far to reach, say, "Please pass the salt."
- Salt and pepper are passed together, like they're married, and passed to the right, counter-clockwise.

Hot Tip: All food passes to the right, counter-clockwise. The only exception is if someone is a few places away to the left.

Cutting Your Food

- Hold the food still with your fork and cut with a knife.
- Point the fork downward with your index finger on the back of the fork where it curves.

- Cut behind the backside of the tines of the fork, below where your index finger holding the fork is pointing.
- Cut no more than three pieces of food at a time (you are not a slicer 'n dicer).
- After cutting your food, place the knife on the plate and transfer your fork to your dominant hand (your right hand, if you are right-handed).
- When drinking or talking and not eating, place your knife and fork in the "resting position." Knife is placed at the top of the plate and the fork with tines up is placed near the center of the plate.

American Style
Resting

Hot Tip: Remember, once you have used a utensil it never touches the table again.

Mind Your Manners

- Take small bites and chew with your mouth closed.
- Don't talk with a mouth full of food.
- Bread or roll is buttered over the bread plate not in mid-air. Tear off a small piece and use the butter you have already placed on the plate.
- Should you need to remove bone or gristle from your mouth, using your thumb and index fingers take it from your mouth and place on the rim of the plate. Don't put it in your napkin.
- If you think something is caught in your teeth, simply say, "Excuse me," and go to the restroom where you can remove it privately.
- The same goes for blowing your nose or applying lipstick. Do it in the bathroom and not at the table.
- When you are done eating, don't push the plate away from you, wait for the server to remove it.

The Art of Conversation

It's not about the food. It's about the business conversation. Stay focused on business and stay off your cell phone.

Most meals begin with small talk. Safe topics for conversation are the weather, movies, sports, and books. Stay away from politics, religion, and sex including inappropriate remarks or jokes. It may be during the main entrée that you begin discussing business. It just depends on how much time you have to meet.

Cells phones are more than user friendly. They're also germ friendly and typically carry more bacteria than the handle of a toilet.

- Keep your cell phone off the table, away from the food, turned to silent or vibrate . . . silent.
- The only exception is if you are on duty and could be called for a 911 life-threatening or emergency situation.
- Alert your guest or host that you may get an important phone call or that you are on duty during the meal.
- When such a call comes say, "Excuse me," and step away from the table to a hallway or somewhere that you can have privacy. Not the restroom. Using a phone in a restroom violates the privacy of others. Besides, your phone doesn't need any more germs!

3 - Ending the Meal

Leaving a meal graciously is as important as eating it graciously. Knowing how to position your utensils demonstrates to your guest and your server you know business etiquette.

- When finished, place your knife and fork on your plate diagonally, pointing from the 4 o'clock position toward the 10 o'clock position.
- Your knife's cutting edge should face toward 6 o'clock.
- Place your fork between the knife and the 6 o'clock position.
- Loosely fold your napkin and put it on the table to the left side of your place setting. This signals your server that you are finished.

American Style
Finished

- Do not ask for a doggie bag. If your host insists on sending you home with a dessert or special item from the restaurant, accept it graciously.

If You are Hosting the Meal
- Choose a restaurant that offers silverware, china plates and cloth napkins. Style counts.
- Be sure to comply with department policies on such issues as alcohol purchases.

- Order something that is easy to eat. Avoid foods like fried chicken, spaghetti, ribs, or spinach salad.

The person who extended the invitation pays. The check is not a tug-of-war situation. If you set up the meeting, you pay.

Hot Tip: If you are the host, arrive early and ask your server to hold the final check and you will pay after your guest leaves. Provide your credit card if requested. This prevents the tug-of-war.

Your department may have budget guidelines on tipping. Check them and comply with the policy. Be sure to give an appropriate tip. Remember, you are representing the fire service.

- Breakfast – 15%
- Lunch – 15 - 20%
- Dinner – 20 - 25%
- If your business lunch has lasted more than an hour, and your server could have served another group in that time, add another 10 percent to your tip.
- When possible let your server know when you sit down that you expect your

meeting to last a while and that you will "take care of" him or her.

- If your server was especially helpful, tell the restaurant manager. Your server will remember you the next time you come in and provide excellent service again.

Chapter in Review

Your success begins before the meal. Know your role and duties whether you're an invited guest or the host. You are representing the fire service so be the savvy professional you are.

Think of your place setting as a B-M-W, which represents bread, meal, water or wine, the order of items from left to right.

Mind your manners. It's the little behaviors and actions you take that show your dining savvy and professionalism.

After your meal, be sure to follow through with a note of acknowledgement to your guest or host to thank them for their time.

Hot Tip: If you would like additional information on the continental style of eating, more dos and don'ts on dining, tips on international dining, or how to eat various foods, go to www.actwelldowell.com to download the .pdf or email marla@actwelldowell.com.

THE TRANSITION TO MANAGEMENT

If you've taken the time to read through the entire book, you now know exactly what it takes to make the transition from the firehouse up the management ladder to Fire Chief.

Over time, continue to think of your transition to new and different positions as having five phases: overcoming anxiety, building self-confidence, being comfortable, developing self-esteem, and accelerating productivity and effectiveness.

Phase One is the state of the unknown where the newly promoted person usually starts. Not knowing or understanding the expectations of management, adjusting to a new group of team members, acclimating to the management culture, taking on new responsibilities, and not knowing what they don't know but they need to know! This can create a level of anxiety.

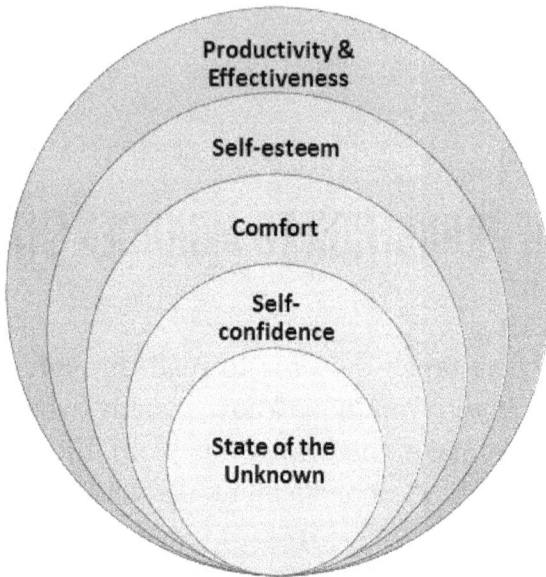

Phase Two is when an individual identifies where they believe change needs to occur. It's being motivated to make changes that move one towards building their self-confidence.

Phase Three is the comfort zone where they become more at ease with their role and responsibilities within the department and organization. It's having confidence in oneself and one's abilities. Self-confidence becomes evident through their performance and behavior.

Phase Four is about self-esteem. It's being confident in one's own merit as a unique, individual; feeling that they can do things well and that people respect them.

Phase Five – enabled with self-esteem and confidence the individual is catapulted into this phase which results in an increase to their own productivity, effectiveness and professionalism.

Good manners and professional behavior always trumps inappropriate conduct in any business, social or personal situation. Be aware, motivated, and courageous to make the changes that are required for success.

I've tried to make this a book of helpful hints. Please use it as a guidebook and know that change doesn't happen overnight. My hope is from time to time you'll refer back to it as a tool to help you navigate your way through the phases of transition. From the firehouse to a polished Fire Chief!

Wishing you the very best in your career.

ABOUT THE AUTHOR

Marla Harr is the owner and chief consultant for Business Etiquette International, a
company whose goal is to help others master
the soft skills and techniques of business
etiquette and protocol intelligence so they can
achieve a competitive edge through the art of
diplomacy. Certified and trained through the
Protocol School of Washington® and backed
by more than three decades of corporate
management and educational development
experience, she brings to her work a mixture of

both entrepreneurial spirit and corporate professionalism.

After working in the corporate arena for many years, Marla started her own meeting and event company, experiencing first-hand the challenges of career transition and learning a new industry's culture and language. It was her mastery of these challenges and her love for helping others to excel professionally that led her to opening Business Etiquette International in 2007.

Her work with the fire service includes presenting at the International Association of Fire Fighters conferences in 2011, 2013, and 2016 speaking at the adjunct program ALTS, and for the State of Ohio in 2014. Her workshops deal with transitioning from the firehouse to a leadership role and working with outside groups such as city councils, mayors, and fundraisers.

Marla is an adjunct faculty member at Arizona State University and California State University. She is also an active candidate member of National Speakers Association - Arizona chapter.

To see how you or your firehouse might benefit from Marla's services you may contact her at: marla@actwelldowell.com

Visit her website at www.actwelldowell.com

ACKNOWLEDGMENTS

International Association of Fire Fighters who have welcomed me as a guest speaker at their annual conference over the years.

The fire fighters who attend my sessions, are always open to learn something new, and make me feel like part of their training team.

Caren Cantrell, my editor, for her patience and expertise.

Cynthia Adkins for developing the title for this book.

Pamela Eyring and The Protocol School of Washington® whose training has been essential to my understanding of proper business etiquette and international protocols.

And my network of family, friends, colleagues, and clients who provided support during the writing of this book.

INDEX

Gratitude, **66**

H

Handshake, **13**, **22**, **23**, **25**, **26**, **27**, **41**, **100**

I

International, **74**, **111**, **134**, **135**, **137**
Introductions, **28**, **30**, **41**, **85**, **115**

L

Listening, **14**, **15**, **18**, **53**, **75**, **79**, **80**, **81**, **86**

M

Meetings, **47**, **89**, **99**, **105**, **111**
Mentee, **55**, **56**, **57**, **60**
Mentor, **8**, **55**, **56**, **57**, **58**, **59**, **60**

N

Noise, **85**

O

Observation, **5**, **51**, **59**

P

Place setting, **118**, **119**, **125**, **128**
Polite, **29**, **37**, **64**, **72**, **97**, **117**
Presentation, **105**, **106**, **107**, **108**, **109**, **111**

R

Receptive, **61**, **80**, **81**, **115**
Relationships, **9**, **18**, **23**, **26**, **37**, **39**, **50**, **55**, **66**, **72**,
    74, **83**

Respect, **39**, **46**, **47**, **49**, **58**, **61**, **62**, **65**, **67**, 77, **95**, **99**, **132**

S

Self-control, 77
Small talk, **37**, **41**, **123**

T

Text message, **69**, **116**

U

Unspoken words, **53**

V

Verbal, **22**, **27**, **66**, **75**, **76**, 77, **78**, **79**, **97**
Voice messages, **13**

W

Work community, **59**
Writing, **13**, **83**, **91**, **92**, **94**, **95**, **98**, 137
Written, **54**, 74, **91**, **94**, **116**